WALKS FOR ALL AGES
LANCASHIRE

WALKS FOR ALL AGES

LANCASHIRE

NORMAN & JUNE BUCKLEY

BRADWELL
BOOKS

Published by Bradwell Books
9 Orgreave Close Sheffield S13 9NP
Email: books@bradwellbooks.co.uk
© Norman and June Buckley 2014

1st Edition

ISBN: 9781902674803

Print: Gomer Press, Llandysul, Ceredigion SA44 4JL

Design by: Erik Siewko Creative, Derbyshire.
eriksiewko@gmail.com

Photograph Credits: © June Buckley
Front Cover Photograph: © Kevin Eaves

Maps: Contain Ordnance Survey data
© Crown copyright and database right 2014

Ordnance Survey licence number 100039353

WALKS FOR ALL AGES

INTRODUCTION

THE NORTHERN PART OF THE LARGE COUNTY OF
LANCASHIRE INCLUDES SOME OF THE MOST ATTRACTIVE
WALKING COUNTRY IN BRITAIN, ALL THE BETTER FOR
BEING LESS WELL KNOWN (AND LESS CONGESTED) THAT THE
NEARBY LAKE DISTRICT AND YORKSHIRE DALES.

Recognising this quality, there are Areas of Outstanding Natural Beauty and Nature Reserves. For the purpose of this book, 'North Lancashire' is loosely defined as the area between the valley of the River Ribble and the boundary with Cumbria, also including the Fylde peninsula.

The broad valleys of the rivers Ribble and Lune combine with the high moors of the Forest of Bowland, the ever popular Fylde Coast and its rural hinterland to offer a wealth of easy routes well suited to the 'walks for all ages' format.

Both the major valleys are noted for the largely unspoilt charm of their stone-built villages, little changed over the years, and for small towns such as Clitheroe, Whalley and nearby Garstang.

In spite of the necessarily short length of the walks included in this book, considerable variety has been achieved. Circular walks predominate but the use of public transport, including the iconic Blackpool tramway, does allow the odd linear route. As befits the format, the walks are not only short, but avoid prolonged or steep ascents, rock scrambling and difficult footpaths and minimise stiles – truly 'walks for all ages'.

Use is made of sections of designated long-distance trails such as the Ribble Way, the Lancashire Coastal Way and the Lunesdale Walk, whilst the towpath of the Lancaster Canal, which threads its way through North Lancashire, contributes to two of the routes. All are carefully described, with the attributes listed as 'The Basics' at the start. Features of interest along the way are mentioned, some of them depicted in the accompanying photographs. Whilst the route descriptions and the sketch maps should give adequate guidance, the use of the recommended Ordnance Survey map will always add to the appreciation and enjoyment of the countryside being traversed.

Shutterstock / Brian Dicks

SILVERDALE

At the north-western extremity of Lancashire, Silverdale is a most attractive area of outcropping limestone, rich woodland and open countryside, criss-crossed with public footpaths.

During the latter part of the 19th century the village was developed as a quiet seaside resort, noted for the views of Cumbria, across Morecambe Bay. For many years designated as an Area of Outstanding Natural Beauty, Silverdale now has Nature Reserves, both National and Local, and is rich in flora and fauna. The Royal Society for the Protection of Birds reserve at Leighton Moss is of national importance. Although industry was always a minor part of the area, there was a lime works, on the line of this walk, and a copper smelter at nearby Jenny Brown's Point.

Today Silverdale is a quiet, off-the-beaten-track, residential village, popular with walkers and botanists. The circular walk set out below offers a good selection of the area's charms, including the peaceful Hawes Water and a former quarrying and limestone works area, now rich in wildlife. The route passes the railway station, giving the option of travelling by train to and from Silverdale, basing the circuit on the station.

THE WALK

1. Walk to the access road, turning left. Pass a bus shelter to reach a road junction in less than 100 yards. Turn right.

2. In 100 yards turn left, over a stile, with a 'Callan Hall' signpost. Follow the path worn over grass, soon crossing the railway line, over stiles. Enter Gait Barrows National Nature Reserve by a signboard and continue towards Callan Hall. Go through a kissing gate. The obvious path keeps well to the right of the buildings of the hall. Ignore paths to the left; follow 'Permissive Footpath Hawes Water Bridleway'. Hawes Water soon comes into view. Go through a gap in a wall to enter woodland, turning right to take a broad track, gently downhill. Ignore a gate on the right. The track soon bears strongly to the right.

3. At a fork keep left, ignoring a gate on the right. Cross a tiny footbridge over a stream; turn right through a gate to reach a length of boardwalk by the edge of

THE BASICS

Distance: 3¾ miles / 6km

Gradient: Modest ascent overall, no steep gradients

Severity: Mostly level or nearly level walking

Approx time to walk: 1¾ hours

Stiles: Four

Map: OS Explorer OL7, The English Lakes, South Eastern area

Path description: Mixture of hard-surfaced roadways with good woodland and grass paths. One short, slightly awkward, section

Start Point: Car park (GR SD 471760)

Parking: Small National Trust car park at the entrance to Eaves Wood

Public Toilets: None en route (toilets at café)

Dog friendly: Generally on leads

Nearest food: Café at Leighton Moss visitor centre

Hawes Water. After the boardwalk stay with the main path, through woodland, with the swampy land of Hawes Water Moss to the right.

4. Leave the nature reserve at a gate, turning right to rise past a pair of cottages along a surfaced access roadway. Pass more properties. The roadway dips to the right before rising steeply to the left.

5. Before the rise turn left through a gate, to follow a permissive path, rising gently to another gate. Pass an information board and the site of the former Trowbarrow lime works. The excellent track continues through the belt of woodland, rising more steeply before reaching the large area of the former quarry.

6. From the quarry, bear to the right, where a diversity of paths heads south. At a fork do not bear left to rise behind a scarp. Go right, along a comparatively minor path, soon passing an information board before reaching a section made a little difficult by rocks and tree roots. This short section leads to a modern gate and a signpost. Go straight ahead to 'Storrs Lane', gently downhill.

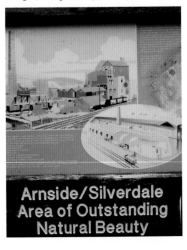

7. Reach the public road through a gate, turning right to walk towards Silverdale village. There is a footpath parallel to the road on the far side which reduces the length of roadside walking. Pass the entrance to Leighton Moss RSPB reserve to reach a road junction.

8. Turn right to walk past the railway station and Silverdale Golf Club. A hundred yards past the station turn left, over a 'Public Footpath, Silverdale Village' signposted stile. There are markers but the traverse of the golf course needs care and an appreciation of the activities of the golf players.

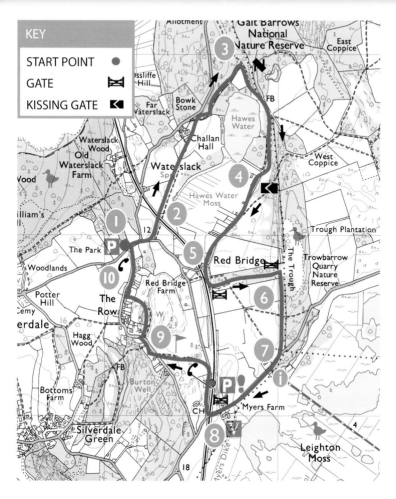

KEY

START POINT ●
GATE ⧓
KISSING GATE ◤

9. Leave the golf course at a gate giving access to a minor lane – The Row. Turn right to follow the road. Descend a little hill, then turn right to take a footpath signposted to 'Dogslack Well'. Stay with this path, passing the well, claimed to be Silverdale's only true well, which formerly supplied water to all the nearby cottages. Go over a stile on the left to rise, going left at a fork and through a waymarked gate to descend and return to the road through another gate.

10. Turn right to follow the lane to its junction with a more major road directly opposite the entrance to the car park.

COWAN BRIDGE

The hamlets of Cowan Bridge, Overtown and Burrow, together with Tunstall Church, are linked by this circuit through the farming land adjacent to the River Leck.

Cowan Bridge has visible remains of the long defunct 'Little North Western Railway', which connected the Settle and Carlisle Railway at Clapham with the West Coast Main Line south of Penrith. There is the site of a Roman fort near Burrow.

In 1824 Revd William Carus Wilson opened a school for the daughters of poor clergymen at Cowan Bridge. He purchased a row of cottages, adding wings at each end. Four of the children of Patrick Bronte of Haworth were sent to this school. For various reasons, including harsh weather and poor food, life was hard for the little girls; so harsh that the two eldest Bronte sisters were taken ill and died soon after their return to Haworth. Conditions at the school were described by Charlotte Bronte in her great novel Jane Eyre, using assumed names for Wilson, the staff and pupils. One of the hardships, particularly in winter, was the Sunday attendance at Tunstall Church, walking in each direction along much the same as the outward route described below. There were morning and afternoon sermons, preached by Wilson, separated by a meagre lunch for the girls, allegedly eaten in the little room above the porch. The school closed in 1833.

The 13th-century Tunstall Church was rebuilt early in the 15th century. The gallery used by the pupils from the school was removed later in the 19th century. The room over the porch remains but, after removal of the gallery, its only access is now by ladder.

Fire, later in the 19th century, destroyed the added wings but the row of cottages in Cowan Bridge remains, end on to the A65. There is a small plaque on the roadside gable.

THE WALK

1. Walk back to the main road, A65; cross the road and take a minor road opposite, signposted to Overtown. Follow this road, nothing more than a country lane, through a generally flat rural area for approximately two miles, passing Harren House and a large building apparently converted into holiday accommodation. The roadside walking is generally pleasant, with very little traffic.

2. Pass through Overtown hamlet, keeping left at a junction to pass Overtown Farm and Moy Park. The road rises at a gentle gradient. Several miles to the left the high

THE BASICS

Distance: 6¼ miles / 10km

Gradient: Gentle and not prolonged ascent totalling 115ft (35m)

Severity: Generally easy walking

Approx time to walk: 3¼ hours

Stiles: Three

Map: OS Explorer OL2, Yorkshire Dales, Southern and Western areas

Path description: A fair proportion of the route is by the side of quiet lanes and the road through Burrow. Paths are generally good

Start Point: Car park (GR SD 636765)

Parking: Small car park behind buildings on the north-east side of A65 at Cowan Bridge Dog friendly: On leads by roadside and through farming land

Public Toilets: None

Nearest food: Highwayman Inn at Burrow. Cowan Bridge Tea Room

ground of Goodber Common is in view. Pass the end of Parkside Farm access drive, the road now skirting a narrow belt of woodland on the right.

3. Two hundred yards after the farm access, as the road bends to the right, turn left to take the right hand of two tracks (not the track leading to Cowdber Farm). Initially the track is a broad, rough, stony roadway, soon passing a large agricultural building, where the roadway ends. There are gates as the route continues the same line; keep close to a fence on the right to pass a stone barn. Ingleborough is in view to the left. The barely visible path goes over grass to another gate. Go over a stile beside a gate, with a battered waymark. Go through yet another gate and over more grass, with Churchfield House and its large outbuildings, apparently converted to holiday accommodation, in view ahead. Descend to a kissing gate and follow a tarmac roadway through the complex.

4. Continue along the access drive. Join a public road, turning right to reach Tunstall Church in 100 yards. Surrounded by a trim churchyard, with attractive trees, the church is beautifully kept and is claimed to be always open to visitors.

5. Leave the churchyard through a little gate behind the church, crossing a large cultivated field (at some times of year a diversion around the edge of the field might be preferred). The right of way heads almost due north, to a little gate at the far end. Cross an overgrown area (a former lane?) to another little gate, almost opposite, with a bridleway waymark. Cross a huge meadow, bearing a little to the left to reach a gate giving access to the main road, A683.

6. Turn right to walk by the roadside, to the hamlet of Burrow. Pass the Highwayman Inn, cross the River Leck and continue past the gates of Burrow Hall.

7. After passing Yew Tree Farm turn right along a farm roadway (not the one leading to the Gamekeeper's Cottage) . Go through the complex of farm buildings, through a gate and along an unsurfaced lane, passing an isolated building. Aim for a waymarked ladder stile over a wall ahead, then stay fairly close to the boundary on

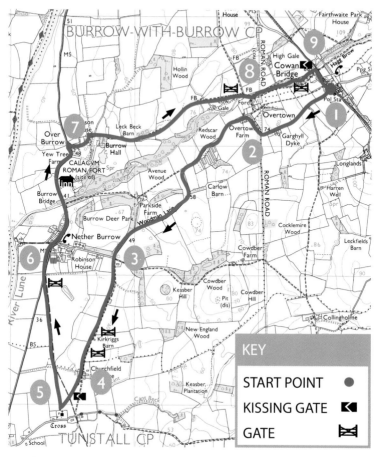

the left of a rising meadow. Go through a gate at the top, continuing close to the fence on the left, with great views to the Pennine Hills ahead.

8. At the bottom do not cross the obvious bridge; go through a gate and bear right to cross the stream a few yards further on. Continue, passing more gates at the side of stock pens. Cross a meadow, bearing right to a gate/ladder stile. Join a surfaced access road, turning left, by the side of the River Leck, very attractive and carpeted with bluebells in May.

9. As the road bends sharply to the left, fork right, along a narrow but clearly defined footpath, staying close to the river as far as the original Cowan Bridge, with weir and pool. Go through a kissing gate and bear left to rise to the road, turning right, over the bridge, to return to the car park.

Monument at Tunstall Church.

Tunstall Church.

HORNBY AND WRAY

CLOSE TO THE CONFLUENCE OF THE RIVERS WENNING AND HYNDBURN AND NOT FAR FROM THEIR JOINING WITH THE RIVER LUNE.

Hornby is an attractive and substantial village of stone-built properties, mainly originating in Georgian times. There is an inn and two or three shops. The church, dedicated to St Margaret of Antioch, is of around 1300, with an octagonal tower of the later 16th century.

Most notable is Hornby Castle; what is now visible, sitting on its mound high above the village, is a 19th-century reconstruction of the ruins of a much older castle. It is not open to the public. The classic view is from Hornby Bridge. During his northern tour in 1816 the great J.M.W. Turner painted a view of the castle, including it in a Lune Valley landscape painting. To the north of the village Loyn Bridge, of 1684, crosses the River Lune; close by is Castle Stede, a motte and bailey castle. Wray is a smaller village, formerly a centre for textiles, with many houses of the 18th century.

THE BASICS

Distance: 3 miles / 4.75km

Gradient: Flat

Severity: Very easy walking

Approx time to walk: 1½ hours

Stiles: None

Map: OS Explorer OL41, Forest of Bowland and Ribblesdale

Path description: Hard surfaced farm road, lane, good footpaths throughout, but some mud in wet weather

Start: Car park (GR SD 586683)

Parking: Public car park at the south-west end of Hornby Bridge

Dog friendly: On leads

Public Toilets: None, but use of the facilities at the Institute in Hornby is permitted

Nearest food: Inns and tea rooms in both villages

HORNBY & WRAY WALK

1. From the car park return to the main road. Cross the road to a wide roadway opposite, with a 'public footpath' signpost. Stay with this concrete-surfaced roadway as it passes old farm buildings before continuing close to the river, soon with views to Hornby Castle to the left. The roadway loses its surface, passing light woodland before bearing right, to a gate. The farm track continues passing isolated farm buildings after which the surface becomes more grassy.

2. Reach and cross the former railway line, with kissing gates on either side. Pass between hedges to a waymarked kissing gate. Go through to follow a 'concessionary path', part of the designated Lunesdale Walk. The path continues along the edge of a field, close to a fence on the left. Go through a gate; the River Hindburn is close on the left. Ignore a stile on the left in 100 yards, heading for the now visible buildings of Wray village ahead. Go through a gate and along a lane, straight ahead to reach houses at the western edge of Wray.

3. At the main road turn left, along the roadside pavement, to pass the road junction at the village centre, bearing left towards Wennington. The inn and the tea room are along the road to the right. Stay by the side of the road as far as Meal Bank Bridge.

4. Go left here, down a roadside ramp to a signpost 'public bridleway'. Turn left to follow the bridleway, between hedges, as far as a redundant sewage works. Go left here, along a broad lane, to rejoin the outward route at a farm gate. Turn right to retrace the route to Hornby.

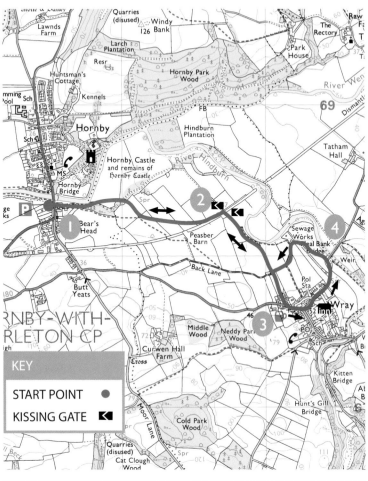

KEY

START POINT ●

KISSING GATE ◤

CATON

JUST A FEW MILES UP THE RIVER LUNE FROM LANCASTER, ON THE NORTHERN FRINGE OF BOWLAND, THE FORMER MILL VILLAGE OF CATON HAS TWO INNS AND A HANDFUL OF SHOPS.

There is now little trace of the cotton and bobbin mills which provided local industry until the 19th century. Unfortunately the main A683 Lancaster to Kirkby Lonsdale road is also the village street. Close to Caton the river has the double bend known as 'Crook o' Lune', painted by the great J.M.W. Turner.

A former railway line which connected west Yorkshire towns with Lancaster and Morecambe has been converted into a cycleway/walking trail. Combined with a riverside path this makes an excellent, easy, level circuit. Although the railway is long gone, the village still has Station Street and the Station Inn.

THE WALK

1. Cross the main road to a little gate with a cycleway signpost. Descend to the former railway line, turning left to walk along the tarmac-surfaced track bed, which is straight, level and pleasantly rural. Cross a minor roadway, then a bridge over Arkle Beck, a tributary of the River Lune.

2. Cross another road; a left turn here reaches the middle of Caton village, with shops and the Station Inn in a few yards. Continue along the former railway line following a 'Crook o' Lune Picnic Site' signpost, passing close to the backs of village properties, crossing a bridge over a minor road and entering woodland.

3. At the point where the line crosses the river, in 2013 a significant construction site blocked the original track descending to the right. A good alternative is provided – turn left for 50 yards, then turn right along a path descending, via a

THE BASICS

Distance: 3¾ miles / 6km

Gradient: Flat

Severity: Easy walking

Approx. min. time to walk: 1¾ hours

Stiles: None

Map: OS Explorer OL41, Forest of Bowland and Ribblesdale

Start Point: Car park (GR SD 542650)

Parking: Substantial free car park/picnic area by the side of the A683 close to Caton village

Dog friendly: On leads

Public Toilets: At car park

Nearest food: Kiosk at car park. Station Inn (short diversion) in Caton village gate, to the river bank. Turn right to pass under the old railway bridge. Continue along a faint path over short grass, close to the river. The views along the shallow valley are quite extensive. The path stays close to the river, passing the occasional kissing gate and a shallow weir before reaching a footbridge over the Arkle Beck. Cross and continue towards Waterworks Bridge and some waterworks buildings, visible ahead.

4. From the buildings continue along the path as it makes a big loop, staying close to the river. If desired a short cut is possible here: turn right by the buildings to follow a narrow path, like a sheep trod, in a fairly straight line cross the neck of the river loop, rejoining the main route in a little less than a quarter mile (half a kilometre). Go through two kissing gates.

4. In a further 40 yards after the second gate turn left at a junction, through a waymarked kissing gate, to follow a broad farm track for a short distance. As the track veers towards the river, go straight ahead over grass, keeping fairly close to the river. As the path approaches the former railway line, there is a badly eroded section beside a stream, leading to a stile. This can be avoided by bearing right a few yards before the difficult section, rising to the fence which separates farmland from the former railway. The fence has been trodden down in at least two places, permitting striding over.

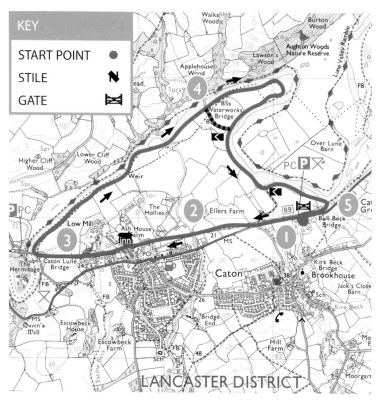

5. Turn right to return to the little gate in approximately 200 yards, then left to cross the road to the car park.

BOLTON-LE-SANDS

PART OF THE LANCASHIRE COASTAL WAY IS LINKED TO THE TOWPATH OF THE LANCASTER CANAL TO PROVIDE A VARIED AND ATTRACTIVE CIRCUIT. WITH THE EXCEPTION OF ONE SHORT LENGTH (WHICH CAN BE AVOIDED) THE TRACKS ARE FIRST RATE THROUGHOUT.

Most scenic is the coastal way, with lovely views of the Cumbrian coast across Morecambe Bay. The canal winds its way above the built-up area of Bolton-le-Sands, well maintained, with beautifully solid overbridges, and with pleasure boats adding to its charm. Ascent is minimal – about 70 feet (20m) over a small headland (avoidable) and a gentle rise of 50 feet (15m) from shore level to the canal.

Apart from one small headland, the eastern coast of Morecambe Bay is flat, a great expanse of sea and sand notorious for trapping unwary cockle pickers and others by its rapidly moving tides and its quicksand. The views to the north are spectacular, the

shore of the Bay backed by the Cumbrian mountains, with the nearer Arnside Knott prominent on the right. A short distance inland, the built-up area of Bolton-le-Sands, with Hest Bank to the south, has an attractive little centre to the east of the main A6 road. The west coast main railway line runs between the built-up area and the sea.

The Lancaster Canal was for some years very successful, linking Kendal with the main canal system at Preston. As with most canals, the advent of the railways greatly diminished the traffic; eventually, during the construction of the M6 motorway, the northern section

was cut off in several places and allowed to become derelict. The southern part is now an attractive waterway for pleasure boating, with a hard-surfaced towpath much used by cyclists and walkers. Traditional farms still graze livestock on the coastal land, supplemented by several caravan sites.

THE WALK

1. Start along a rough roadway, towards a low headland. The Coastal Way, as shown on the Ordnance Survey map, goes over the headland but it is evident that a well-worn track bears left to pass below the headland (at least when the tide is not too high!). This variation avoids two stiles. For the official route bear right to  a gate/stile. Keep close to the fence on the left of the rising field; the path is indistinct. The views across the bay are extensive. Descend to a stile, pass a few static caravans and through an old farm.

2. The two tracks now join together. There is a minor roadway and a delightful path along the top of a low embankment. The next settlement is Red Bank, where there are seats. Continue along the fine coastal track. As the road turns inland, continue along the track, towards the very obvious Wild Duck Hall, down steps with a waymark and over a section of boardwalk.

THE BASICS

Distance: 4½ miles / 7.25km

Gradient: No significant ascent

Severity: Easy

Approx time to walk: 2¼ hours

Stiles: Ten (Eight can be avoided)

Map: OS Explorer 296, Lancaster, Morecambe and Fleetwood

Path description: Excellent canal towpath; very good along the Lancashire Coastal Way: final section indistinct across fields (with stiles) but can be avoided if desired

Start Point: Car park. (GR SD 471676)

Parking: Free parking near Morecambe Lodge Caravan Site. Accessed from A5105 Hest Bank to Morecambe road, via a minor road (Pilgrim Lane)

Dog friendly: On leads (possibly loose along part of the Coastal Way)

Public Toilets: None en route

Nearest food: Royal Hotel, Bolton le Sands accessed directly from the canal towpath

3. Join a surfaced road, bearing left towards the Hall. Bear right in front of the Hall and follow the road inland towards Bolton-le-Sands, passing under the railway line to reach a residential area. Keep straight ahead (roadside pavement) to rise gently to the A6 main road.

4. Cross (carefully!) towards a little group of shops. Take the minor road passing to the right of the shops (Whin Grove). This soon becomes a lane, rising gently to a wooden gate on the right.

5. Turn right at the gate to join the canal towpath, turning right to follow the towpath winding above the Bolton-le-Sands built-up area. Part way along is the inviting beer garden and rear entrance to the Royal Hotel. After several bridges, pass under the A6 road, a wider bridge, to reach the Hest Bank swing bridge. In a further quarter mile (half a kilometre) look out for a descending flight of steps, with waymark.

6. Turn right, descend the steps and follow a narrow passage between fenced gardens to reach the main Morecambe road (A5105). Cross over, turn left, and follow the roadside pavement for approximately 200 yards.

7. Turn right, through a kissing gate, to take a signposted route across a field. There is no clear path; bear well to the right to reach a small waymarked footbridge, with stiles, across a ditch. Cross a narrow field to another little bridge, with stiles. Rise towards a footbridge across the railway line, with ladder stiles at each end. Turn right towards a caravan site, over two more ladder stiles and follow the instruction to walk close to the field boundary as far as a wooden gate. Go through the gate, pass farm buildings, go through another gate and join the coastal path. Turn right to return to the car park.

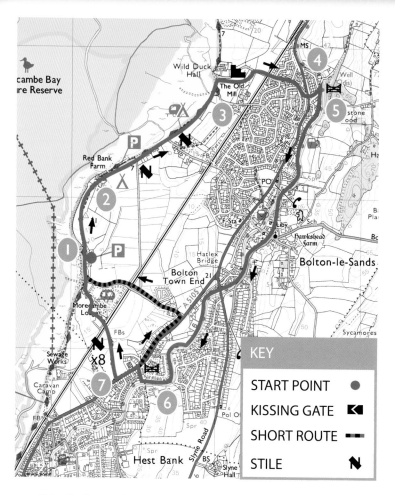

KEY

START POINT ●

KISSING GATE ◪

SHORT ROUTE ▬▬▬

STILE ◣

Note: The last section of the walk, from the A5105, contains eight stiles and probably some mud underfoot. If desired, this section can be avoided by turning right after crossing the road and walking along the roadside pavement as far as Pilgrim Lane (a little less than half a mile), which gives vehicular access to the car park. Turn left to walk along the lane direct to the car park.

MORECAMBE & HEYSHAM

A VIRTUALLY LEVEL WALK MAINLY ALONG THE SEASIDE
PROMENADE CONNECTING MORECAMBE WITH ITS NEAR
NEIGHBOUR HEYSHAM.

The only ascent, at Heysham, is very modest
and, apart from a few yards up to St Patrick's
Chapel, there is tarmac underfoot throughout.
Sea views are constant and the view approaching
the mound of Heysham Head, with a cluster of
white cottages, is most appealing. The return to
Morecambe is by bus (route no. 4).

Morecambe was for many years a thriving
traditional Lancashire seaside holiday town.
Unlike Blackpool, it lost most of its visitors some
years ago when the overseas package holiday
boom took hordes of holidaymakers from the Lancashire and Yorkshire towns to warmer,
drier and more exotic destinations. In recent years valiant efforts have been made to
attract visitors; floral decorations, sculptures and the refurbishment of the iconic art
deco Midland Hotel are among the more obvious. Arguably Morecambe's finest feature

Shutterstock / Tom Curtis

is the view across the bay to the
Cumbrian coast, backed by the
southern mountains of the Lake
District. The sunsets can be
superb.

Heysham is notable as an Irish
Sea ferry port. There is also an
attractive old village on the edge
of what has become a large built-
up residential area. At Heysham
Head the renowned historic site
includes the ruins of St Patrick's
Chapel, with several rare 'stone
coffins' hewn into the solid rock.

THE WALK

1. The promenade, cycleway and walkway are accessed directly from the car park. Turn left to walk south, towards the Midland Hotel, passing the lifeboat station and the end of the stone jetty. Bear left to pass close behind the hotel, noting various sculptures and a 'Heysham 2' signpost. Continue along the wide promenade. To the left is the Morecambe Superbowl. There are plenty of seats as the promenade heads towards Heysham.

THE BASICS

Distance: 2¾ miles / 4.5km
Gradient: Almost flat
Severity: Easy walking
Approx time to walk: 1½ hours
Stiles: None
Map: Ordnance Survey Explorer 296, Lancaster, Morecambe and Fleetwood
Path description: Hard-surfaced promenade, followed by roadways in Heysham
Start Point: Car park (GR SD 430645)
Parking: Large seafront pay and display car park approximately 300 yards north of the prominent Midland Hotel, Morecambe
Dog friendly: On leads
Public Toilets: Near the Midland Hotel, along the promenade and close to the bus stop at Heysham
Nearest food: Midland Hotel, Morecambe. Royal Hotel and choice of cafes in Heysham

2. Pass the Battery Hotel, a small car park and a jetty and continue. There are various circular signs on the ground, including 'West End Pier' and a curious comparison of the body of water included in Morecambe Bay with Niagara Falls. Pass another signpost. Part of the old village comes attractively into view ahead. Pass a children's play area.

3. The promenade forks. Keep right, along the lower walkway, now narrower, just above the beach/sea. Go up steps on the left, into the village, passing a tea garden before joining a public road.

4. Turn right to follow Main Street. To visit the ancient site turn right by the church, rising along a broad roadway with a sign board on the wall, pass a small parking area and reach the ruins, a fine viewpoint. Return to Main Street, turning right to descend, passing cafés before reaching a large open area with information centre operated by the National Trust.

5. Adjacent is a bus stop with turning circle and timetable, including route no.4. Return to Morecambe; there is a bus stop close to the entrance to the car park.

Shutterstock / Kevin Eaves

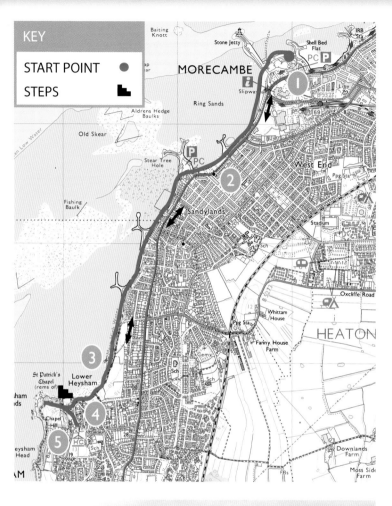

KEY

START POINT ●

STEPS

GLASSON

Part of the Lancashire Coastal Way is combined with paths and minor roads to link the old port of Glasson with the (scanty) ruins of Cockersand Abbey.

Once a bustling port, created when it was apparent that larger vessels could not readily reach the quays at Lancaster, further up the River Lune, Glasson is now a shadow of its former self. It retains some of its historic maritime interest; the large dock is still evident and there is a great basin used as a marina by pleasure boats. The basin is the terminus of a branch of the Lancaster Canal.

Not much remains of the once powerful Premonstratensian Cockersand Abbey (constructed about 1190 and vacated in 1539) but it does provide a focal point along the Lancashire Coastal Way, a delightful track on the vast shore of Morecambe Bay. The countryside is entirely agricultural, mainly grazing land.

THE BASICS

Distance: 5 miles / 8km

Gradient: Almost level

Severity: Easy walking

Approx time to walk: 2½ hours

Stiles: Two

Map: OS Explorer 296, Lancaster, Morecambe and Fleetwood

Path description: Good path along the coast, minor road and field paths to return

Start Point: Car park (GR SD 446561)

Parking: Huge car park adjacent to the extensive basin at Glasson

Dog friendly: Generally on leads, some release might be possible on the Coastal Way

Public Toilets: Adjacent to car park

Nearest food: Inns and cafés at Glasson

GLASSON WALK

1. Leave the car park, turning left to pass the Victoria Inn and crossing over the lock between basin and dock. Continue along the street, gently uphill. At the top of the hill (Brodie Hill) is a view indicator and a road junction.

2. Turn left to follow the roadside footpath, downhill. As the road bends to the left, turn right, along Marsh Lane, surfaced as far as the entrance to a caravan site. Continue along the lane, through two gates and then cross a huge meadow, the path now not very distinct. Aim roughly towards distant farm buildings but bending left then right to cross a watercourse on a bridge. Head towards the buildings.

3. Go through a gate at Crook Farm, bearing left up to a signpost to reach the shore. Follow 'Lancashire Coastal Way' to the left. The track is initially hard surfaced, close to the stony/sandy beach. Ahead, to the right is Plover Point, with a little lighthouse; far away to the left is the high ground of Bowland. As the roadway bends left, inland, at a cottage keep right to pass a small car park, the track now becoming unsurfaced. After an information board and a kissing gate the path becomes narrower but is still excellent, with profuse wild flowers. After another kissing gate leave the path, bearing left to a cluster of buildings, including the remains of Cockersand Abbey, with information board.

4. From the Abbey pass through a gate, over a stile and to the left of a derelict farmhouse. Go right then left to follow a vehicular track across the fields

5. Go through a gate to join a public road, keeping left. Bear right at a road junction, staying with the minor road for approximately one mile, with several sharp bends. Ignore 'footpath' signs on the left.

6. Reach Gardner's Farm, a large collection of buildings on the left. At the far end of the farm turn left at a 'footpath' sign. Go through/over two gates/stiles, cross a field to another gate and continue with a hedge on the left. After another gate follow a farm drive, pass Kendal Hill Farm, keeping right, indicated by a waymark on a

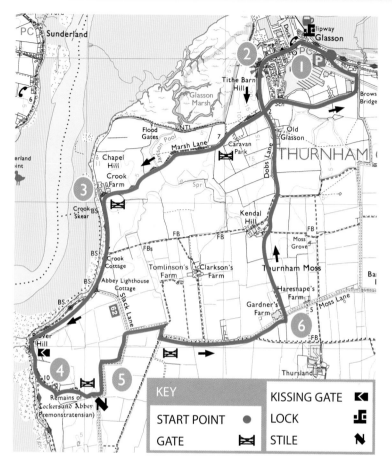

KEY

START POINT ●	KISSING GATE
GATE	LOCK
	STILE

post then left to a gate/ stile. Continue along the edge of a meadow to a gate and a farm access roadway. Stay with the roadway, passing Old Glasson Farm, with huge silos, before rejoining the outward route. There is a choice here, either to retrace the outward route or (better?) to turn right, following the roadside footpath to a left turn and a bridge over the canal. Immediately after crossing the bridge descend steps to the canalside towpath, leading directly to the car park.

ABBEYSTEAD

Sitting prettily in the broad valley of the River Wyre, a mile or so from the road which connects Lancaster with Clitheroe through the Trough of Bowland, the quiet hamlet of Abbeystead provides a focus for an attractive short walk.

Abbeystead has a handful of old stone buildings, largely of farming origin, a school and a large village hall. Adjacent is Abbeystead Reservoir, a widening of the river largely obscured by thick woodland. The nearest church (Christ Church, also named the 'Shepherds' Church') has a splendid site approximately one mile away, on a knoll above the valley.

The circuit set out below, including part of the designated Wyre Way, is well varied, with woodland, farmland and the riverside. It is more demanding (and rewarding) than its modest length would indicate, with a variety of conditions underfoot and a steady ascent of the side of the valley.

I AM THE DOOR OF THE SHEEP.

THE WALK

1. Start along the little road, towards a signpost. Cross a bridge over a tributary river.

2. Turn right immediately along a path, with a little sign on the left and a waymark on a post. The path is never in doubt as it winds its way through the attractive woodland, always quite close to the water of the River Wyre/Abbeystead Reservoir. There are a few steps up and down and possibly wet sections despite a good deal of paving. Reach a stone wall on the left, soon descending gently to the right, with the dam and spillway now close. Descend to reach a footbridge across the river.

THE BASICS

Distance: 3 miles / 5km
Gradient: Total ascent 217feet (67m). Quite prolonged ascent at a steady gradient
Severity: More demanding than average
Approx time to walk: 1¾ hours
Stiles: Four
Map: OS Explorer OL41, Forest of Bowland and Ribblesdale.
Path description: Very varied – narrow, winding and possibly wet through the woodland, Path not visible on ground in crossing grassy meadows. Short length of road through Abbeystead
Start Point: Car parking area (GR SD 564544)
Parking: Small parking area by the side of the river
Dog friendly: On leads through farming land
Public Toilets: None
Nearest food: Inn at crossroads west of Dolphinholme, approximately four miles (6½ km) from Abbeystead

3.   Cross the bridge and rise to a waymarked gate/stile ahead. Bear left to a concrete roadway. Follow this roadway along the side of the valley, passing substantial buildings. Leave the roadway to continue the same line on a broad, unsurfaced track, with a waymark on a post. Go through a waymarked gate. Fifty yards after the gate, leave the broad track, forking left to follow a narrow path across a huge meadow, keeping a straight line with the river close on the left. Angle slightly right to ascend a low bank and aim for a gate, rejoining the wide track just before the gate. Go through and follow the track, quite steeply uphill.

4.   Forty yards after the gate look carefully for the start of an indistinct and rugged path on the right which ascends the valley side, always quite close to the fence at the edge of the woodland. At the top the Lentworth Hall farming complex comes into view and there are fine, long views across the valley. After a gate/stile follow the fence to the middle of the farm. Go over a stile and through the farmyard.

5.   Turn right at a waymarked kissing gate at the far end and take a straight line across a huge meadow, initially with a stone wall on the left. At the far end, bear a little to the left, downhill, to reach a gate. Ascend the grassy slope to the church, now visible above. There is a little gate in the churchyard wall, with a carved stone adjacent.

6.   From the church set off down the slope. Avoid the dense rushes, aiming just to the right of a distant cluster of farm buildings (Far House Barn) and keeping about 30 yards away from the fence/ditch on the left. At the bottom of the field go over a stile situated 30 yards to the right of the corner of the field and descend to a footbridge over a stream. Cross the bridge, then cross a meadow towards the buildings of Far House Barn, going over a stile on the way. Go over a stile to the left of the barn. Join a concrete roadway for a few yards.

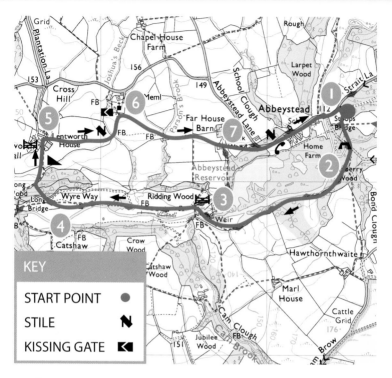

KEY

START POINT ●

STILE ➍

KISSING GATE ◀◀

7. Turn left to leave the roadway behind the barn, descending a little path to a gate. Continue across a small field, aiming for a gate, just to the right of a house. Go through to join the public highway, turning right to descend to Abbeystead hamlet and the car park.

SLAIDBURN

A CIRCULAR WALK AROUND THE RIVER HODDER
COUNTRYSIDE, UPSTREAM OF SLAIDBURN VILLAGE, ON THE
EASTERN SIDE OF THE FOREST OF BOWLAND, WITH GOOD
VIEWS FROM THE HIGHER PART OF THE WALK.

The Forest of Bowland is a large and attractive area of hills and valleys north of the Ribble valley, designated as an Area of Outstanding Natural Beauty since 1964, bounded on the west by Lancaster, the west coast main railway line and the M6 motorway and on the east by the fringe of the Yorkshire Dales. In this context 'forest' has nothing to do with trees – for centuries it was a jealously guarded royal hunting ground, with public incursion also discouraged by subsequent landowners wishing to safeguard their

property, largely for shooting purposes. Fortunately the area is now more walker-friendly. The celebrated 'Trough of Bowland' is the gap in the hills through which the road linking Lancaster with Clitheroe passes.

As principal village of the eastern portion of Bowland, Slaidburn is a focal point for visitors, with inn, shop, stone cottages and cobbled pavement sitting attractively above the adjacent River Hodder. The Hark to Bounty Inn, named after a favourite hound of an important customer, contains a former courtroom, in use for several centuries until 1937.

THE WALK

1. From the car park turn left to walk by the roadside to the bridge across the River Hodder. Cross, then turn left immediately at a 'public footpath' sign, go over a stile and follow a path close to the riverside, soon passing through light woodland, rising gently. Go through a waymarked kissing gate to rise across a field, bearing a little to the right. Go through a waymarked squeezer stile, cross a stream on a sleeper

THE BASICS

Distance: 2¼ miles / 3.5km

Gradient: Approximately 300 feet (90m) of ascent, no steep gradients

Severity: Moderate

Approx time to walk: 1¼ hours

Stiles: Two

Map: OS Explorer OL41, Forest of Bowland and Ribblesdale

Path description: Much of the route is over short grass, with paths indistinct but not too difficult to follow. One slightly boggy area

Start Point: Car park, Slaidburn village (GR SD 714524)

Parking: Pay and display car park at the edge of Slaidburn village

Dog friendly: On leads

Public Toilets: At car park

Nearest food: Café adjacent to car park. Hark to Bounty Inn, Slaidburn village

bridge and continue the same line across the next rising meadow, heading for a gap in the wall ahead, at a junction of walls. Continue, soon across more level ground, with trees to the left. Pass a waymark on an electricity pole and go through a gateway; the track is better defined but the ground becomes slightly boggy.

2. Reach a waymarked gate on the right but do not go through; this is a junction of rights of way. Turn sharp left to continue with a well-made stone wall close on the right. As the wall ends bear left, soon reaching a broken stone wall. Keep this wall fairly close on the left, descending a large meadow to reach a waymark on a post and a gate.

3. Go through the gate to continue the descent to Bell Sykes Farm along a sunken lane. Go through a waymarked gate to pass through the farm. Leave the farm to walk along the unsurfaced farm access roadway, leading to Holmehead Bridge, reached through a gateway, then a small gate, both waymarked.

4. Cross the bridge. In 100 yards go left to leave the roadway at a waymark, by the end of a wall. The route stays close to the wall, over short-grazed grass. Go through a kissing gate, soon reaching Croasdale Brook. Go to the right, as indicated by a waymark, rising to a gate giving access to a public road.

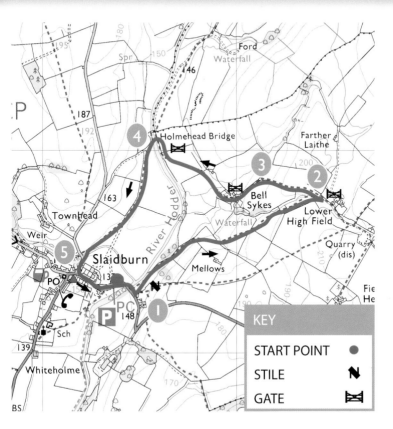

5. Turn left, cross the brook on a bridge and reach the village centre at the war memorial. Turn left to descend to the car park.

BOLTON-BY-BOWLAND

A RELATIVELY EASY CIRCULAR WALK LARGELY THROUGH
AGRICULTURAL LAND, BASED ON ONE OF THE FINEST
VILLAGES IN THE RIBBLE VALLEY.

Two ancient greens, with stone cross and stocks, lie at the heart of Bolton village. Part of the Bolton Hall estate, on the south-eastern fringe of Bowland, Bolton has been protected from modern development for more than a hundred years. The result is a stone-built village of considerable charm, a short distance to the north of the River Ribble. The church of St Peter and St Paul is 15th century. Inside, the famous Pudsey tomb has the figure of Sir Ralph Pudsey in full armour, together with his three wives and their twenty-five children. The site of the former Bolton Hall is close to Bolton Hall Farm, where the site of 'King Harry's Well' is marked by a circular building.

THE WALK

1. From the car park turn right to walk along the village street, passing the Coach and Horses Inn and rising to the church of St Peter and St Paul.

2. Turn right at white gates between stone pillars to pass a 'private road – access only' sign and follow a tarmac drive, initially with a fine avenue of trees, for more than half a mile (nearly 1km) towards Bolton Hall Farm. At the crest of a slight rise is the stone base of a former cross on the left. Immediately before reaching a

THE BASICS

Distance: 3 miles / 5km

Gradient: Total ascent approximately 80 feet (25m)

Severity: No steep hills

Approx time to walk: 1½ hours

Stiles: None

Map: OS Explorer OL41, Forest of Bowland and Ribblesdale

Path description: A surfaced roadway, meadows without distinct paths and a short distance by the side of a quiet public road. Crossing the grazing land needs care with route finding

Start Point: Car park, with information room (GR SD 785495)

Parking: Small car park close to Skirden Bridge

Dog friendly: Definitely on leads, likely to be grazing livestock

Public Toilets: At the car park

Nearest food: Café close to the car park

group of cottages look over a gate on the right to see the circular building marking the site of King Harry's Well.

3. Opposite the cottages turn left to rise along a stone cobbled roadway. At the crest of the rise turn left through a gate with a 'public footpath' sign. Continue across a large field, reasonably close to the right-hand boundary, to reach a kissing gate. Cross the next, larger, field on much the same line, well above the woodland which lines the adjacent bank of the River Ribble. Cross a mini bridge over a stream; bear right, with a fence on the left. In a few yards turn left through a little gate and continue across a third meadow, initially with woodland close on the right. This meadow is long and narrow. Approaching the far end keep well to the left to rise and exit along a narrow but clear track leading to a kissing gate. Follow a grass track with a fence on the right to another waymarked kissing gate and continue along the edge of a meadow towards a building, ahead. Go through a kissing gate on the right and pass to the right of the buildings of Fooden farming hamlet. Go through a gate on the left, down a few steps, and bear left to pass through the hamlet.

4. Leave Fooden by rising between buildings and going diagonally across a small field. Continue close to the right edge of a much larger field; Pendle Hill is in view to the left, the fringe

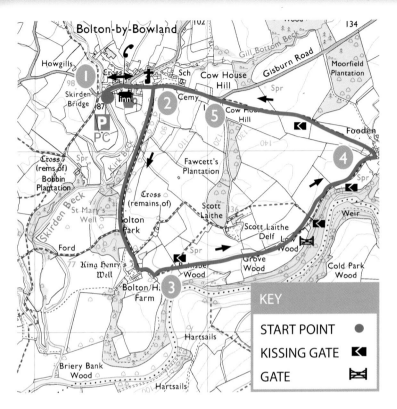

of the Bowland Hills ahead. Go through a waymarked kissing gate in the top right corner and continue, as indicated by the waymark, now downhill with Bolton village in view ahead. There is another kissing gate and another field. Follow a line

of trees, aiming well to the right of a prominent building, to reach a kissing gate giving access to the public road.

5. Turn left to walk by the roadside back to the village, rejoining the outward route at point 2 to return to the car park.

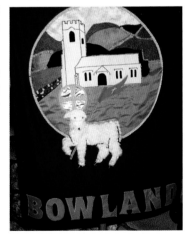

CLITHEROE

A circular walk largely by the River Ribble linking two bridges on the fringe of Clitheroe, with ascent limited to approximately 80 feet (25m).

The return passes through the grounds of Waddow Hall, notable as a training and activity centre for the Girl Guide movement. An interesting feature is the option to add a sculpture trail.

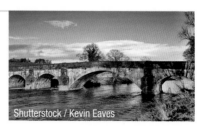
Shutterstock / Kevin Eaves

A small market town of character and charm, according to some commentators Clitheroe is the 'finest in Lancashire'. Streets of individual small shops, inns and cafés are crowned by the 800-year-old castle on its great mound. The castle museum and the platform gallery at the railway station are particular features of the town.

Waddow Hall was originally a mill owner's mansion. Low Moor was the site of Clitheroe's first cotton spinning factory of 1782, surrounded by millworkers' cottages early in the 19th century. The mill eventually grew to house more than a thousand looms. The mill was demolished in the 1960s but some of the cottages remain. Most of the large site has been developed for modern housing.

The sculpture trail extends from close to Brungerley Bridge to Crosshill Quarry. It was created in 1993 by Thompson Dagnall.

THE WALK

1. From the car park cross the road at a pedestrian crossing, towards a sporting complex. Pass between an indoor swimming pool and a tennis centre. As the road comes to an abrupt end, continue over grass to a 'Ribble Way' sign at the edge of woodland. Turn right to follow a narrow path along the edge of woodland, soon reaching another marker. Go through a gap between houses to join an estate road, bearing left; as the road bends to the left there is another 'Ribble Way' marker. Go straight ahead; there is another sign. Do not go left at 'Riverside'. Former millworkers' cottages are evident and the former Wesleyan School of 1866 is passed.

2. The route soon becomes a rough-surfaced track, passing a building development site and above allotment gardens to reach a waymarked kissing gate. There are paddocks with ponies and donkeys, part of a stud farm.

THE BASICS

Distance: 2¾ miles / 4.5km. Sculpture trail adds ½mile / 1km
Gradient: Steady but not steep ascent from Brungerley Bridge to Waddow Hall
Severity: Generally easy walking
Approx time to walk: 2½ hours
Stiles: None
Maps: OS Explorer OL41, Forest of Bowland and Ribblesdale
Path description: Roadways and good paths, 2 sets of steps which require due care
Start Point: Car park (GR SD 728414)
Parking: Large pay and display car park on the town side of Eddisford Bridge
Dog friendly: On leads
Public Toilets: Close to each of the bridges
Nearest food: Picnic area with café close to Eddisford Bridge. Wide selection (off route) in Clitheroe town

3. After the gate leave the broad track, up a bank on the right, to another waymarked gate. Continue along the elevated path, now with fine views, including Clitheroe Castle, to a post with several waymarks. Bear left to descend to the river bank, taking care with the wide, shallow steps en route. Go through a kissing gate, cross a little footbridge and ascend the stone steps up to the road, at the end of Brungerley bridge. To add the sculpture trail to the walk, turn right for a few yards, cross the road, and turn left through a gate, one of the two entrances to the trail. There are boards giving information.

4. For the basic route, or after including the trail, cross the bridge and follow the roadside pavement, uphill, as far as a waymarked kissing gate on the left. Go through the gate to follow a good, rising, surfaced track through the grounds of Waddow Hall. Go straight ahead at a crossing and continue, with the Hall below to the left, following 'deliveries only' as far as a cattle grid. Turn right here at a waymark and 'public footpath' sign to follow a little path around the perimeter outbuildings. After a gate, reach a broader track, heading away from the buildings, to cross fields and reach the public road, through a kissing gate.

5. Turn left to walk by the roadside for half a mile (1km), with Pendle Hill in view. Pass the Shireburn Caravan Site before descending to a signposted footpath and footbridge across the River Ribble.

6. Cross the bridge and turn right, by the riverside, before rising to rejoin the outward route and returning to the car park.

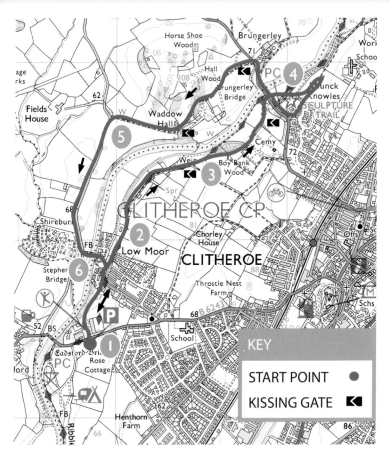

KEY

START POINT	●
KISSING GATE	◤

Shutterstock / Kevin Eaves

Clitheroe Castle.

A motte and bailey castle built on a natural carboniferous limestone outcrop.

Shutterstock / george green

HURST GREEN & STONYHURST

A SHORT CIRCULAR WALK WHICH TRAVERSES THE GROUNDS
OF THE OUTSTANDING STONYHURST COLLEGE, LINKED WITH
ADJACENT AGRICULTURAL COUNTRYSIDE. STONYHURST HAS
LONG BEEN A GREAT FOCAL POINT OF ROMAN CATHOLICISM
IN NORTHERN ENGLAND.

Formerly the stately home of the resolutely
Catholic Shireburn family, building commenced
in the 13th century, with gradual replacement
and enlargement over a period of 250 years.
After an 18th-century change of ownership
the house was allowed to decay before being
offered to the Jesuits and transformed into

a boarding school for Catholic boys. Further extensions were carried out, resulting in
Stonyhurst becoming one of Britain's most eminent schools. One of the additions is St

Peter's Church of 1835, built as a replica of
the chapel at King's College, Cambridge. The
author J.R.R. Tolkien had a close association
with the school, living in a guest house in
the grounds whilst writing The Lord of the
Rings. He also worked in the college itself. Sir
Arthur Conan Doyle was a pupil at the college.
Stonyhurst is occasionally open to the public
during the summer holidays.

An attractive stone-built village with three inns and other facilities, Hurst Green is situated
close to Stonyhurst and to the Ribble Valley. There is an elegant former almshouse
building.

THE BASICS

Distance: 2 miles / 3.25km

Gradient: Approximately 50ft (15m) ascent, very gentle

Severity: Easy walking

Approx time to walk: 1¼ hours

Stiles: None

Map: OS Explorer 287, West Pennine Moors

Path description: Tarmac roadways and good grass path

Start Point: Car park (GR SD 685382)

Parking: Car park in front of village hall, towards northern end of Hurst Green main street

Dog friendly: On leads

Public Toilets: Near centre of Hurst Green

Nearest food: Three inns and café in Hurst Green

HURST GREEN WALK

1. Turn right to walk up the village street, heading towards woodland.

2. Turn right at Smithy Row, reaching a footpath at the far end of the Row. Go through a kissing gate and continue over short grass along the left edge of a field, with Pendle Hill in view. Go through another gate and head towards an isolated building. After another waymarked kissing gate, cross a little valley, with stream, bearing right towards a fence, with the college buildings some way ahead and a rugby field on the right.

3. Go through a gate to join a college roadway. Turn left to reach the church by a road junction. To view the great south-east frontage of the college divert to the right for a hundred yards. Return to the junction. Keep to the left of the church to follow the roadway round to another road junction in front of the college.

4. Turn left, with large ponds to each side of the road, to follow the very straight road, rising steadily but gently. The ponds have plentiful waterfowl.

5. Pass between rugby pitches; at the far end of the straight road, the monument 'Ave Maria' stands on a mound. Follow the road to the left, straight into Hurst Green and the car park.

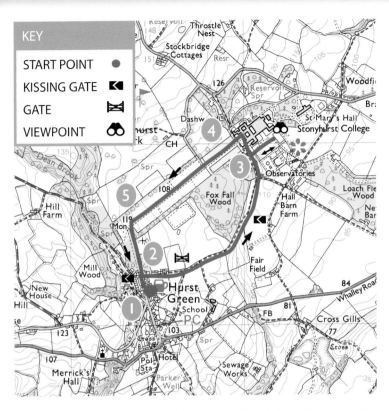

KEY

START POINT ●

KISSING GATE ◄

GATE ⋈

VIEWPOINT 👓

LONGRIDGE FELL

A RARE OPPORTUNITY FOR A LARGELY CIRCULAR WALK ACROSS HIGH MOORLAND, LARGELY HEATHER AND RUSHES, REACHING THE SUMMIT OF THE FELL, WHICH IS EASY ENOUGH TO QUALIFY FOR INCLUSION IN A 'WALKS FOR ALL AGES' BOOK.

A variation through woodland on the return, adding nearly half a mile and a little ascent, is possible.

Detached from the great mass of the Forest of Bowland hill country, Longridge Fell, makes an impact greater than might be expected from its modest 1150ft (350m) height.

Largely because of its detachment it is a great viewpoint, from the present route particularly to the north towards Chipping and the Hodder valley. The peak, 'Spire Hill' on Ordnance Survey maps, is crowned by an elevated trig point.

Much of the high ground of the fell is covered by forest. The town of the same name is several miles to the south, small and of no particular distinction.

THE BASICS

Distance: 3 miles / 5km

Gradient Total ascent 260 feet (80m), all at gentle gradients

Severity: No steep hills

Approx. min. time to walk: 1¾ hours

Stiles: One

Map: OS Explorer OL41, Forest of Bowland and Ribblesdale

Path description: Largely a typical moorland path, in part rough and stony underfoot. Short length at side of quiet road

Start Point: Car park (GR SD 640402)

Parking: Generous lay-by at Jeffrey Hill

Dog friendly: Yes - open moorland

Public Toilets: None

Nearest food: None en route. Half Drop Inn, a little more than one mile (1½ km) along the road in the direction of Ribchester

LONGRIDGE FELL WALK

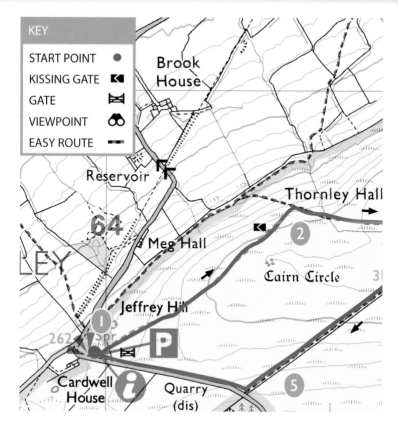

KEY

START POINT	●
KISSING GATE	◪
GATE	⋈
VIEWPOINT	⚭
EASY ROUTE	▬ ▬

Brook House

Reservoir

Thornley Hall

64

Meg Hall

Cairn Circle

Jeffrey Hill

262

Cardwell House

Quarry (dis)

1. From the south-eastern end of the lay-by go through a gate, signposted 'concessionary footpath', to start along a very clear track across the moorland, rising gently and passing a waymark on a stone. Pass an upright stone. The path becomes narrower, passing a stone cairn and through a boggy area with dense growth of rushes.

2. Reach a 'T' junction with a major path. Turn right to continue the gentle ascent, heading for the edge of woodland.

3. At the next 'T' junction turn left, now with a wall and woodland on the right. Go over a waymarked stile and continue, passing a track joining from the left, soon reaching the top at Spire Hill with its trig point, a fine viewpoint.

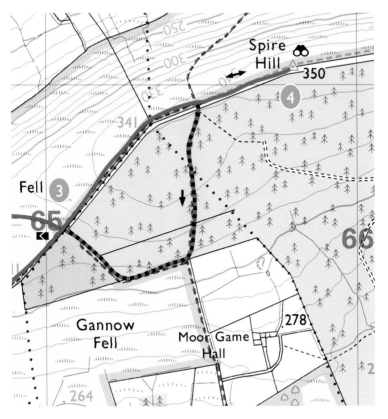

4. Return along the same track. In less than a quarter mile (½ km), at a gate, it is possible to turn left, then bear right, in line with a redundant stile, to descend through woodland, soon bearing right at the south edge of the woodland, then right again to return to the main track at point 3. Without the variation, continue to point 3. Go straight ahead, still with the wall on the left and with views to the south, across the Ribble valley. There are lengths of rough path; heading for the right edge of a plantation.

5. Go through a signposted gate to join the public road. Turn right, initially uphill, to return to the parking lay-by.

BEACON FELL COUNTRY PARK

A CIRCUIT WITHIN A COUNTRY PARK, THIS IS A CHARMING WALK WITH INTERESTING FEATURES AND WITHOUT SERIOUS ASCENT.

At the western fringe of the Forest of Bowland, the Beacon Fell Country Park was established as long ago as 1969, covering a largely wooded hill of modest height (873 feet or 266m).

The park is criss-crossed by established trails, mostly colour coded. The visitor centre is open daily, with information and with educational facilities for visiting groups.

The summit of the hill can be readily reached from the centre. The walk set out below circumnavigates the hill, avoiding the ascent to the summit. There are long views in several directions.

THE WALK

1. Start by walking up a cobbled track by the side of the café, towards a large sculpted head. Bear left along a gravelled path through the woodland.

2. At a fork turn right to ascend, not very steeply and not for very long. Go straight ahead at a cross paths, through a gap in a wall, into more open country. Cross a tiny stream before rising again, soon reaching a fearsome sculpture

THE BASICS

Distance: 2 miles / 3.25km

Gradient: Several short ascents

Severity: No steep gradients

Approx time to walk: 1¼ hours

Stiles: None

Map: Ordnance Survey Explorer OL41, Forest of Bowland and Ribblesdale

Path description: Good paths and woodland tracks throughout

Start Point: Visitor centre at Beacon Hill (GR SD 564426)

Parking: Fellside car park at the visitor centre. Access to the country park is best from the A6 main road, turning east at a signposted junction one mile south of Garstang

Dog friendly: On leads

Public Toilets: At visitor centre

Nearest food: Bowland café at visitor centre

3. By the sculpture keep right at a junction, still rising gently. Keep left at another junction, with a cattle grid on the right. Keep straight on at the next junction, then right at a fork, with a 'T' (tracker) sign. There is a signpost for 'The Tarn and Black Tiger Wood'. Go straight across a surfaced roadway.

4. The charming little tarn, with seats and picnic table, is now evident to the left, reached by a short diversion from the route. To continue, follow the gravelled path on the right. At a 'T' junction turn right. At the next junction go up to the right for a few yards, then go left, along a track signposted to the Bowland Visitor Centre. There are more visitor centre signs as the track bears right, uphill, now a broad avenue through the trees, soon with the centre in view ahead.

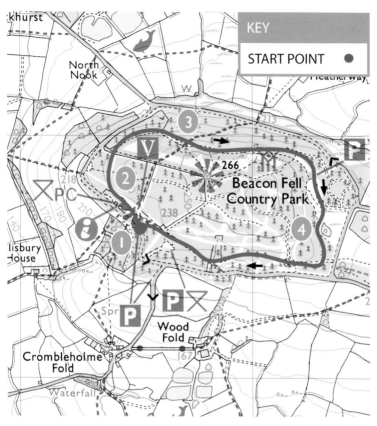

GARSTANG

Happily by-passed by the A6 main road, Garstang is a pleasant small town, its main street containing numerous small shops, with inns, cafés and a former town hall of ancient origin.

There is also a Discovery Centre. Bounded by the River Wyre on the east, bisected by the Lancaster Canal and with the hills of Bowland rising just a few miles away, Garstang has a fine situation.

Borough status and a market charter date from the reign of Charles II; the market is still held each Thursday. The former town hall originated in 1755. Although twice rebuilt following fires, the present structure has retained a pleasing Georgian elegance.

CORN MILL

A Fulling mill existed here in the 13th century to process cloth from Cockersands Abbey Estate. The later corn mill's wheel was housed horizontally in the basement and the route of the leat can still be seen nearby.

LOTTERY FUNDED

The Lancaster Canal has a sizeable basin close to the town centre, with a former tithe barn, older than the canal, beside. There are moorings for visiting boats. The Wyre Aqueduct, carrying the canal 30 feet (10m) above the river, is a fine piece of canal engineering by the great John Rennie.

The gaunt remains of Greenhalgh Castle stand on a knoll a little way to the east of the town. Built by the first Earl of Derby in 1490 and holding out against Cromwell's forces during a siege in 1645–6, it was one of the last Royalist strongholds in Lancashire.

This short but interesting circuit includes part of the long-distance Wyre Way, canal towpath, a rural track close to the castle ruin and, if desired, part of the attractive Garstang main street.

THE BASICS

Distance: 3 miles / 5km

Gradient: Almost flat, apart from the 30ft (10m) (steps) rise from river to canal

Severity: Easy walking

Approx time to walk: 1½ hours

Stiles: Two

Map: OS Explorer OL41, Forest of Bowland and Ribblesdale

Path description: Surfaced Wyre Way and canal towpath, a little minor road, one small meadow without path

Start Point: Car park (GR SD 492454)

Parking: Large signposted pay and display car park, close to town centre

Dog friendly: On leads

Public Toilets: At car park

Nearest food: Several inns and cafés on main street in Garstang

GARSTANG WALK

1. Go to the far end of the car park, close to the river, to join the Wyre Way, a surfaced footpath, signposted to the Lancaster Canal. Turn right to follow this excellent path, above the river. Join a roadway into the built-up area, following the roadside pavement to the main street, Bridge Street, bearing left to cross the road bridge.

2. Turn right immediately to descend to 'Cornmill', now a care home. There is a 'Wyre Way and Lancaster Canal' signpost. Go through the mill archway to follow a narrow riverside path as far as the aqueduct.

3. Bear left, up flights of steps (with handrail) to reach the canal towpath. To view the town basin turn left towards Lancaster for approximately 200 yards. Retrace steps to point 2 and continue along the towpath, passing numerous moored boats, many of them adaptations of traditional narrow boats. Pass a fine old milestone – 'Lancaster 13, Preston 17' – as the canal skirts the fringe of Bonds residential area. Waterfowl such as mallard and swans are plentiful. Pass under several numbered bridges.

4. At Bridge 56, leave the canal, ascending steps (with handrail) and over a stile, to cross the bridge and follow a broad track between hedgerows. In not much more than 100 yards go through a gate and turn left immediately, over a waymarked stile and a plank bridge across a ditch. Cross a small meadow without path, aiming for large farm buildings. Pass through gates, with the buildings on the left, and continue

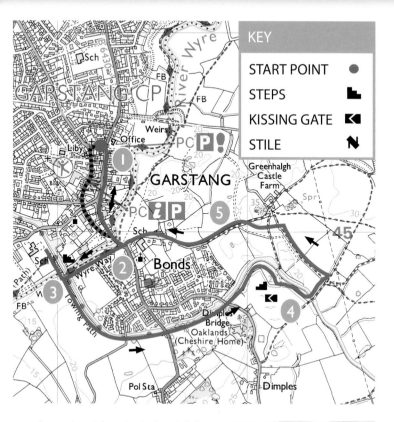

KEY

START POINT	●
STEPS	⌐
KISSING GATE	◄
STILE	ᚅ

along a broad farm track. Bear left to stay with this track as it passes below Greenhalgh Castle Farm and the knoll with the castle ruin. Go through a gate to join a surfaced farm road. Across the way is an information board and the best view of the castle ruin.

5.   Turn left, downhill, soon reaching houses on the Garstang fringe. Join the main street close to the river bridge, turning right to rejoin the outward route at point 2. Either retrace that route via the Wyre Way footpath or (recommended) follow the main street with its refreshment opportunities, shops and town hall, as far as the entrance to the car park.

KNOTT END-ON-SEA

FORMERLY A FISHING SETTLEMENT, THEN A MINOR COASTAL HOLIDAY RESORT, KNOTT END-ON-SEA IS NOW AN OFF-THE-BEATEN-TRACK RESIDENTIAL AREA, SITUATED IN THE ANGLE BETWEEN THE COAST AND THE ESTUARY OF THE RIVER WYRE.

There is a pedestrian ferry link to Fleetwood and a small shopping centre. To the north there are long views across the extensive waters of Morecambe Bay. On a clear day the southern Lake District fells, including Black Combe near Barrow-in-Furness, are visible. For many years there was a railway branch line connecting Knott End to what is now the West Coast Main Line, near Garstang. Locally it was affectionately known as the 'Pilling Pig' purely because the line passed through Pilling and an early locomotive had a whistle uncannily like the howl of an anguished pig.

The Wyre estuary is now generally limited to pleasure boating; until the mid 19th century several small ports were comparatively busy and there was some shipbuilding. The construction of Fleetwood and its docks ended this period of activity, with Fleetwood becoming a great ferry and fishing port. In its turn, Fleetwood has now lost most of its trade and the salt marshes of the estuary have become important nature reserves.

South of Knott End, the extraction of brine and rock salt from the area around Preesall, linked to the large ICI chemical works across the estuary, has left its marks on the landscape, primarily ponds and depressions in the fields. Hackensall Hall dates from 1656, with extensive renovation in the 1870s. Small parts of the Lancashire Coastal Way and the Wyre Way are included in this circular walk.

THE WALK

1. Leave the car park, bearing right, along the seafront esplanade, with long views across Morecambe Bay; there are seats and shelters along the way. As the accompanying road bends inland, keep straight on to follow a good track, part of the Lancashire Coastal Way.

2. After approximately one mile (1½ km), just short of a static caravan site, turn right to descend a lesser path, cross an access roadway and continue on a narrow path along the side of a residential development. The path has a ditch alongside before reaching a roundabout. Go straight across

THE BASICS

Distance: 4 miles / 5km
Gradient: Flat
Severity: Easy walking
Approx time to walk: 1½ hours
Stiles: Three
Map: OS Explorer 296, Lancaster, Morecambe and Fleetwood
Path description: Good paths, some hard surfaced but some mud is possible
Pavement beside one length of residential road
Start Point: Car park (GR SD 345485)
Parking: Large free car park close to the ferry terminal at Knott End
Dog friendly: On leads
Public Toilets: At car park
Nearest food: Bourne Arms, Knott End

and follow the roadside pavement for approximately a quarter mile (½ km) to reach the Knott End main access road. Go straight across towards the visible war memorial opposite. Go through a gate and over a stile beside the memorial to follow a narrow footpath over grass, towards woodland.

3. In approximately 200 yards, at the near end of the wood, go over a stile on the right to continue through the wood. At the far end of the wood go over another stile to join a farm track. Turn right to stay with this broad track through fields, ignoring a footpath on the right. Join an unsurfaced roadway, with a white farm to the left; bear right, through woodland.

4. Go left at a junction, passing Hackensall Hall on the left. Bear right to pass golf course buildings. There is a 'Knott End' signpost. Cross the golf course on a good track. Follow a waymark to pass two houses, before turning left along a waymarked little path to reach a signpost and the Wyre Way, along the side of the estuary. Turn right to follow the surfaced top of the sea wall, past the golf clubhouse, directly to the car park.

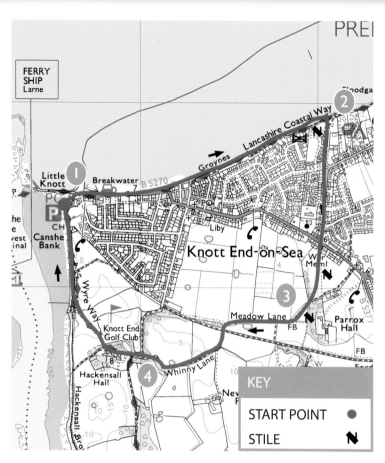

KEY

START POINT ●

STILE ⋏

The Lancashire Coastal Way provides an excellent linear walk along the seafront, passing Rossall Point.

The recommended and convenient return is by the Blackpool tramway. The port at Fleetwood is still operational, although it is a shadow of its former self. In the earlier part of the 19th century it was a great trading port and also the most important fishing port on the west coast. After construction of the branch railway line in 1840, it became a convenient gateway to Scotland, Ireland and the Isle of Man. At the same time, the town was developed from a cluster of cottages to a fashionable seaside resort by Peter Hesketh-Fleetwood, owner of a vast local estate. It is still quite attractive, renowned for its indoor and outdoor markets and, like the Fylde coast generally, for its extensive beaches and its bracing sea air.

Rossall Point is marked by a modernistic building, facing out to sea. This stretch of coast, the southern boundary of the vast Morecambe Bay, is noted for large flocks of birds roosting and feeding.

The Blackpool tramway is truly iconic. A lone and popular survivor of the 19th-century tramways which covered all major cities until the mid 20th century, it has recently (2012) undergone a total refurbishment, with elegant modern trams running from Starr Gate to Fleetwood Ferry, a total of 11 miles.

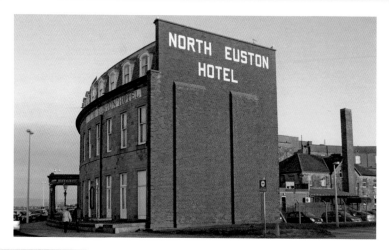

THE WALK

1. Start along the Esplanade, heading away from the North Euston Hotel, passing the Marine Hall and gardens, soon forking right at a brick-built ice cream kiosk to keep close to the sea. There is a little 'Lancashire Coastal Way' sign. Pass a boating lake on the left and a 'Rossall Point 360m' sign, with the building now in view.

THE BASICS

Distance: 4 miles / 6.5km

Gradient: Flat

Severity: Easy level walking

Approx time to walk: 2 hours

Stiles: None

Map: OS Explorer 296, Lancaster, Morecambe and Fleetwood

Path description: Mainly promenade, part of the Lancashire Coastal Way, plus a good field path

Start Point: The Esplanade, Fleetwood, near the North Euston Hotel (GR SD 336485)

Parking: Roadside spaces on the Esplanade

Dog friendly: On leads

Public Toilets: Signposted, close to the North Euston Hotel

Nearest food: Choice of hotels, cafés, ice cream kiosks close to the parking area

2. At Rossall Point there are public conveniences behind the buildings and a golf course inland. Continue along the coastal way, now heading south; the large and diverse buildings of Rossall School come into view. The original house was the home of the Hesketh-Fleetwood family, developed as an independent school from 1884. Blackpool Tower can be seen (a long way) ahead.

3. As the school is approached look carefully for a left turn to a waymarked footpath, pass a gate and continue on a good path along the edge of a large field, with the school buildings to the right. Pass another gate, reach a road, and pass tennis courts and a few houses before bearing right then left to reach a main road at traffic lights. The Rossall School tram stop is immediately to the right.

4. Stay with the tram to its terminus at 'Fleetwood Ferry'. This is at the Esplanade. Go to the left, through gardens, to pass the North Euston Hotel and return to the parking area.

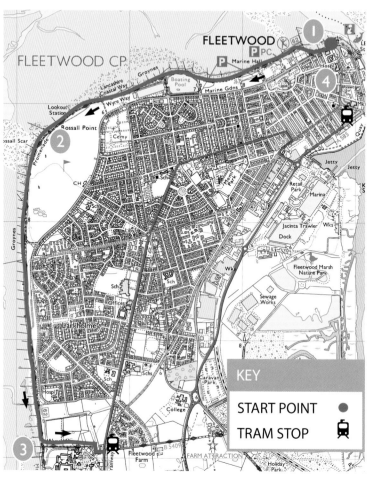

KEY

START POINT	●
TRAM STOP	🚊

WYRE ESTUARY COUNTRY PARK

AN EASY LITTLE CIRCULAR WALK IN AN OFF-THE-BEATEN-TRACK PART OF LANCASHIRE, BY THE SIDE OF THE ESTUARY OF THE RIVER WYRE.

Recognising the importance of the potential recreational use of the area around the estuary of the R. Wyre, the Wyre Estuary Country Park was conceived in the late 1980s. A site at the former minor port of Stanah was chosen as the focal point for the park and work commenced to improve footpaths, plant trees, construct a visitor centre with café and install seats and picnic tables. The country park was opened in September 1991. With its abundant wildlife, particularly waterfowl, parts of the estuary, particularly the salt marshes, had already been designated as nature reserves.

From as early as the 16th century small ports at Skippool and Wardleys had traded with Russia, the Baltic and America and there was a shipyard at Wardleys. The creation of Fleetwood in the 1840s ended the viability of these ports.

Adjacent to the present Cockle Hall picnic area was a small cottage known as Cockle Hall, allegedly occupied by a family of thirteen at the end of the 19th century.

THE BASICS

Distance: 2 miles / 3.25km
Gradient: Almost flat
Severity: A very easy walk
Approx. min. time to walk: 1 hour
Stiles: None
Map: OS Explorer 296, Lancaster, Morecambe and Fleetwood
Path description: Excellent track and a short length of footpath beside a minor road
Start Point: Wyre visitor centre (GR SD 356432)
Parking: Substantial car park adjacent to Wyre visitor centre
Dog friendly: On leads
Public Toilets: At visitor centre
Nearest food: Wyreside Café, at visitor centre

WYRE ESTUARY WALK

1. Head away from the café, along a roadway at the edge of the car park for 60 yards, to the start of a footpath, with signpost. Go along the footpath, soon passing a children's play area on the right.

2. Bear left, cross a road and take the lower path, with sign boards, closest to the estuary, soon reaching a small picnic area, Cockle Hall, at a junction of paths. The path continues, close to the estuary, with plenty of seats and views across the water to Hambleton and upstream towards Skippool.

3. After a long right-hand bend, at a junction of paths keep right, leaving the estuary. There is a waymark on a post. Reach a surfaced minor road. Turn right, rising gently to Stanah House Farm. Turn left, along Stanah Road.

4. On reaching the visitor centre access road, River Road, turn right to walk along the roadside footpath to return to the car park (the café is up a few steps on the right).

These enclosures have been planted with native trees to increase the diversity of habitats in the area. Wildflowers and other natural vegetation have been allowed to proliferate to encourage butterflies and other fauna to become established locally.

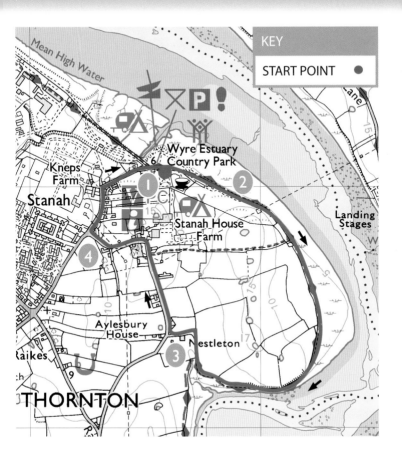

KEY

START POINT ●

STANLEY PARK

ALTHOUGH CLOSE TO THE CENTRE OF BUSY, BUSTLING, BLACKPOOL, STANLEY PARK IS A LARGE, PEACEFUL AREA. EVEN MORE SURPRISING IS THE APPARENT REMOTENESS OF MARTON MERE, A WILDLIFE SANCTUARY.

This walk connects the two, using roadways within the park, a large meadow, well-established paths and grass sward to provide an unusual and interesting route.

Situated on the eastern fringe of the Blackpool conurbation, Stanley Park has long had a reputation as one of the finest of the great municipal parks. Extending to 256 acres, it was largely designed by the legendary Thomas Mawson. Opened in 1926, the park includes Italian and rose gardens, a memorial clock tower, an extensive boating lake and sporting facilities including Blackpool Cricket Club. The café occupies an art deco building.

Marton Mere is a Site of Special Scientific Interest. A sizeable lake, its open water and reed beds are noted for populations of varied water fowl which can be viewed from several hides.

THE WALK

1. From the visitor centre walk past the café, heading for the visible clock tower and the circular Italian garden, with fountain. Bear left, down a few steps. Continue in the same direction; below, to the left, is the bandstand and one end of the boating lake. Pass tennis courts on the right then fork left at a junction to reach a visible major public road in a short distance.

2. Cross the road at pedestrian traffic lights a few yards to the right. Turn right, along the roadside footpath, looking carefully for a little path leading to a gap in the fence on the left, giving access to a large field. The gap is opposite the model village visitor attraction. There is no path on the ground; the Ordnance Survey shows a right of way in a straight line across the field.

THE BASICS

Distance: 3½ miles / 5.5km

Gradient: Flat

Severity: Easy level walking

Approx time to walk: 1¾ hours

Stiles: None

Map: OS Explorer 286, Blackpool and Preston

Path description: Well-established path around the mere; hard-surfaced walkways in Stanley Park; one grassy meadow without path

Start Point: Visitor centre at Stanley Park (GR SD 327359)

Parking: Large parking area adjacent to the visitor centre in Stanley Park

Dog friendly: On leads (there are populations of water fowl and other wildlife around the mere)

Public Toilets: At the Stanley Park visitor centre

Nearest food: Large café, with outside terraces, at the visitor centre

STANLEY PARK WALK

3. Reach a surfaced roadway at the far edge of the field. Turn left to follow the roadway, soon bending strongly to the right. The roadway loses its hard surface before a gate/kissing gate is reached. This is the entrance to the Marton Mere SSI.

4. Turn right immediately after the gate, along a clear path.

5. At the next kissing gate there is an information board with a large-scale map of the area and a signpost. Turn left, along a narrow path, soon reaching a caravan site on the right. There is now no path; walk along the left edge of mown grass, with the mere occasionally visible close on the left, passing two hides. As the adjacent caravan site road bends to the right, go straight ahead, past a children's play area.

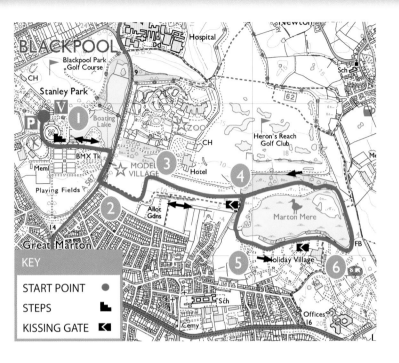

KEY

START POINT	●
STEPS	⌐
KISSING GATE	◤◀

6. At a 'public footpath' signpost turn left to follow a stony path. Cross a bridge and stay with this excellent path as it bends round the mere, passing more hides, and keeping left at the only significant junction. Rejoin the outward route at point 4. The return through Stanley Park can be varied if desired.

LYTHAM WINDMILL

A GENTLE LINEAR STROLL ALONG THE LANCASHIRE COASTAL WAY, LINKING FAIRHAVEN LAKE VISITOR CENTRE WITH THE PROMINENT WINDMILL AND LIFEBOAT MUSEUM AT LYTHAM.

The coastal way is officially along the surfaced promenade, but the latter part of the walk can be on adjacent grass areas if preferred. The recommended return is by a convenient bus service.

Lytham is an ancient settlement, founded and controlled for many years by a Benedictine monastic cell. After purchase by the Clifton family in 1606, development into the present sizeable residential area proceeded steadily. Lytham and the more recent (late 19th-century) Ansdell and St Anne's have merged to form a large residential area separated from Blackpool by the airport. Lytham docks enjoyed 19th-century prosperity until a new dock at Preston took trade further up the Ribble Estuary.

Shutterstock / Alastair Wallace

Standing on the grass expanse between town and sea, the windmill is a notable feature. From 1805 until wrecked by a storm and subsequent fire in 1919, it was a working mill. Restored in 1989, it is now a visitor attraction, open during the season (but not usually on Mondays or Tuesdays). Close by is the old lifeboat house, also a museum open to the public. Fairhaven Lake is a large and attractive sheet of water, with varied boating, sporting and other visitor facilities.

THE BASICS

Distance: 3 miles / 5km

Gradient: Flat

Severity: Entirely level

Approx time to walk: 1½ hours

Stiles: None

Map: OS Explorer 286, Blackpool and Preston

Path description: Surfaced promenade

Start Point: Fairhaven Lake visitor centre (GR SD 340274)

Parking: Parking area at Fairhaven Lake visitor centre. Accessed from the coastal road, approximately 1¾ miles (3km) south-east of St Anne's pier

Dog friendly: On leads

Public Toilets: At visitor centre and at far end of lake

Nearest food: Café at visitor centre. Inns and cafés at Lytham

Shutterstock / Alastair Wallace

You may wish to extend the walk to St Anne's Pier by walking up the south promenade.

LYTHAM WINDMILL WALK

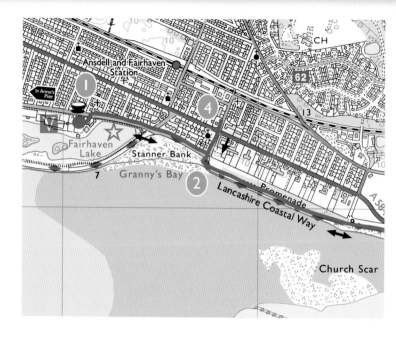

1. Pass the café and the Ribble Discovery Centre and continue along the track by the side of the lake. At the end of the lake, with more public conveniences, rise to join the roadside footway. Walking and cycling routes are painted on the ground.

2. As the road (Ansdell Road South) goes to the left, turn right. The route is now straightforward, along the surfaced promenade. To the left there are tracks through the scrubby grassland, eventually over cut grass, heading for the obvious windmill.

3. Reach the windmill and the adjacent Lifeboat Museum. Turn round to retrace your steps as far as a car parking area/roadway. Turn right, cross the road and continue along Dicconson Terrace as far as a pedestrianised area. Round the corner to the right are bus stops. Route 7 (15-minute intervals) provides a swift return to the Fairhaven Hotel, close to the lake.

4. Walk along the road beside the hotel for 120 yards to reach the outward route close to the end of the lake. Turn right to return to the visitor centre.

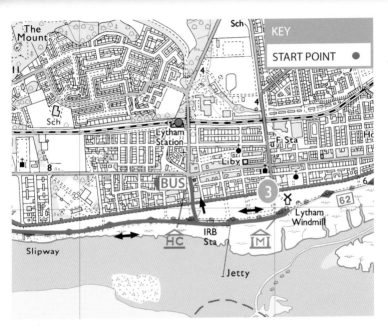

KEY

START POINT •

ABOUT THE AUTHOR

Following a professional career in environmental health, in partnership with his wife, June, Norman Buckley commenced writing guide books, mainly but not entirely footpath guide, in the early 1990's.

Almost forty books have so far been published, covering areas in the United Kingdom and Western Europe. A speciality has been the popular 'Level Walks' series. Over much of the same period, Norman and June have worked as walking consultants for a major holiday organisation.

Revelevant interests include photography, travel, railways and industrial archaeology Norman holds a Diploma in Environmental Management (Liverpool University) and a Master of Arts Degree in Lake District Studies (Lancaster University). The author is a member of the Guild of Outdoor Writers and Photographers.

Norman and June have lived in the Lake District since 1990.